DENTAL CARE

LIFE GUIDES

DENTAL CARE

Brian R. Ward

Series consultant:
Dr Alan Maryon-Davis
MB, BChir, MSc, MRCP, FFCM

LIFE GUIDES

Franklin Watts
London · New York · Toronto · Sydney

© 1986 Franklin Watts

First published in 1986 by
Franklin Watts
12a Golden Square
London W1

First published in the USA by
Franklin Watts Inc.
387 Park Avenue South
New York, N.Y. 10016

First published in Australia by
Franklin Watts Australia
14 Mars Road
Lane Cove
New South Wales 2066

UK ISBN: 0 86313 402 5
US ISBN: 0-531-10179-7
Library of Congress Catalog Card No: 85-52044

Design: Howard Dyke

Picture research: Anne-Marie Ehrlich

Illustrations:
John Bavosi, Dick Bonson, Howard Dyke,
Sally Launder.

Photographs:
B & C Alexander 15
British Dental Museum 39
Sally & Richard Greenhill 7, 45
London Hospital (Dental School) 19, 20, 29, 34, 37
Ann Ronan Picture Library 42
Sporting Pictures UK Ltd 43r
John Watney 39, 41, 44
ZEFA 30, 35, 43l

Printed in Belgium

Contents

Introduction

Tooth care is part of looking after your body. It takes only a few minutes each day to keep your teeth and **gums** looking healthy and attractive. If you brush your teeth regularly and take care to eat the right foods, there is no reason why you should not be able to keep your teeth for a lifetime.

What is the alternative? What happens if you don't take care of your teeth? Teeth are very conspicuous, and if you neglect them, it will soon be obvious to others that you don't care about your appearance or mouth hygiene. Discolored and decaying teeth are unsightly, but before this sort of damage occurs there will be problems with bad breath, which is unpleasant for others.

If teeth are not cleaned properly, tooth **decay** can soon develop. **Cavities** and toothache will follow unless you receive proper dental treatment. Gum disease is common too if mouth hygiene is neglected. This is not only painful, but it can lead to tooth loss. Eventually tooth neglect means that dental repairs will be necessary, and finally **dentures** may be required to replace missing teeth.

A middle-aged man with all his teeth has something to smile about. Until quite recently most adults had lost the majority of their teeth well before middle age and had to wear dentures.

▷ Care of the teeth begins in childhood, which is when the teeth are most at risk from decay. Learning to care for your teeth while still young should mean that you will keep your teeth healthy for the rest of your life.

Looking at teeth

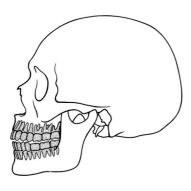

The teeth are firmly rooted in the bony jaw, which supports them so they can be used to bite and chew your food.

We develop two sets of teeth during our lifetime. The first are the **milk**, or deciduous teeth, which develop soon after a baby begins to grow in its mother's womb. When the baby is born, about twenty of the milk teeth have formed, but are not yet visible.

There are also a few of the adult or permanent teeth present at birth, and these are positioned underneath the milk teeth, waiting to develop years later. The milk teeth usually start to push their way through the gums at around six months of age, starting with those at the front. By the time the child is three, all twenty milk teeth have usually appeared.

Teeth continue to grow throughout childhood. Permanent back teeth (**molars**) start to appear without disturbing the milk teeth at about the age of six years. But up to the age of about twelve the adult teeth continue to emerge through the gums, pushing out the milk teeth as they develop. The last of the thirty-two adult teeth to appear are the large molars at the back of each jaw. These may not emerge until the late teens and are known as **wisdom teeth**.

▷ In a child's jaw the milk teeth appear first through the gums. But below these, even before birth, are the adult teeth (shown in blue), developing like small seeds until they are ready to push out the milk teeth, one at a time.

▽ Teeth are used for different purposes, depending on where they are positioned in the jaw, The **incisors**, at the front, are for cutting. The **canines** behind them are for piercing or tearing food. **Premolars** and molars are powerful grinding teeth which we use for chewing.

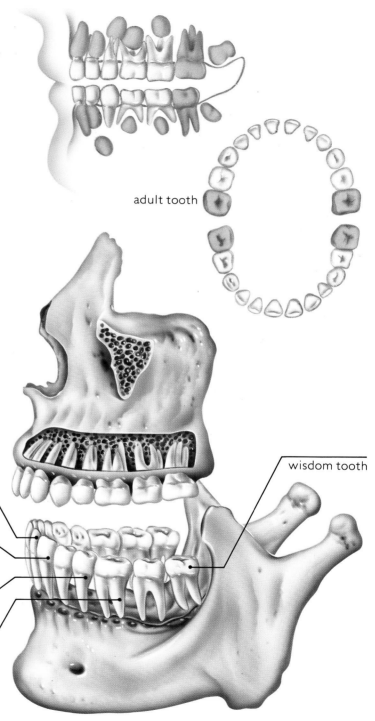

adult tooth

wisdom tooth

incisor

canine

premolar

molar

9

The living tooth

A tooth is a living structure, composed of a hard substance resembling bone. The outer layer is called **enamel**. This covers all the part of the tooth that appears above the gum. Enamel is a very hard white material which protects the tooth from damage. It makes up the grinding and cutting surfaces which are important when we eat.

Beneath the enamel is the slightly softer **dentin**. This yellowish material is identical to the ivory of an elephant's tusks, and it makes up most of the tooth. Both enamel and dentin are mostly made up of **calcium** salts, which though very hard, can be dissolved by **acids**.

Dentin extends right into the **root**, where the tooth is secured in the jaws. Inside the dentin is the **pulp cavity**, which runs into the root of the tooth. The pulp cavity contains blood vessels which bring **oxygen** and nutrients into the tooth. It also contains **nerves**, which allow us to feel sensation through the tooth. This prevents us from biting so hard that we cause damage. Nerves make us aware of hot or cold foods and also warn us when decay has penetrated into the tooth.

A cross-section of a molar
tooth. Its **crown** of enamel is
very hard and resists wear,
while the dentin underneath
is softer and can be easily
damaged by decay. Dentin in
the root is covered by a layer
of material called cementum.

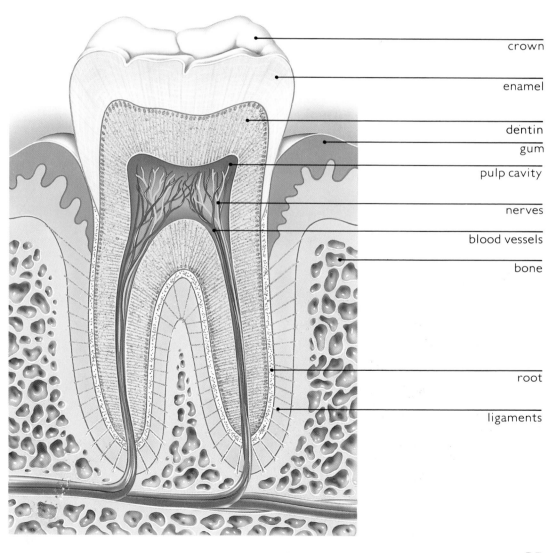

crown

enamel

dentin

gum

pulp cavity

nerves

blood vessels

bone

root

ligaments

Biting and slicing

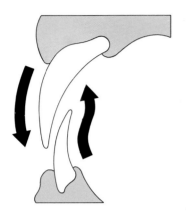

The teeth at the front of the mouth are specialized for particular tasks. At the very front are the incisors. There are four in the top jaw and four in the bottom. They are spade-shaped and flattened and have a single root. When you close your jaw, they slide across each other like the blades of scissors, cutting and slicing your food. When you bite into an apple, it is the incisors which take out a clean section of the fruit.

△ The flat incisor teeth slide across each other as you bite, just like the blades of a pair of scissors. They are used to cut or slice food.

▽ The teeth of animals are adapted to deal with a particular diet. The enormous canine teeth of this extinct tiger helped it to kill and tear at its prey.

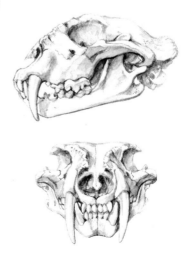

Next to the incisors are the canine ("dog-like") teeth, of which we have four. These teeth are rounded and have a sharp point. They too have a single root. The function of the canine teeth is to hold and tear the food. In many animals, like dogs, tigers and other **carnivores**, or meat-eaters, these teeth are very large. In humans they are not so important, so they are not usually any more prominent than the other teeth. Often the tip of the canine becomes blunted by wear in adults.

Humans have adapted to eat a mixed diet, so we have a combination of the types of teeth needed to eat vegetable material and the canine teeth typical of meat-eaters.

The teeth of a dog are typical of meat-eaters, with very long, sharp canine teeth. In contrast, the rabbit's incisors are long and chisel-shaped to help it to bite off plants. In the sheep, the upper incisors have disappeared. It crops grass by pressing the lower incisors against a tough pad on its upper jaw.

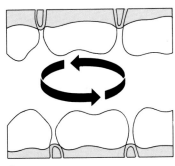

The molar and premolar teeth crush and grind food between the sharp points or cusps on the crowns of the teeth.

Opposite
Although we would not enjoy the experience, this Eskimo is chewing a piece of seal leather to soften it. Our jaws are immensely powerful and can exert enormous pressure.

The chewing teeth

Behind the canine teeth, on each side of both jaws, are a pair of premolar teeth, followed by two, or sometimes three, larger molars. These are the teeth used for chewing and grinding the food, and they are quite different from the teeth in the front of the mouth. The premolar teeth have two pointed projections, or **cusps**, on their surface and one or sometimes two roots. Their main function is for chewing. As the jaw moves up and down, the premolars grind together.

Behind them the larger molars crush and grind the food. These teeth are broad and blunt, with four or more pointed cusps which grind the food against the molars in the opposite jaw. Each molar is deeply embedded in bone with three large curving roots. These are necessary because of the tremendous forces put on the teeth during chewing – as much as 2,500 kg (900 lb) per square cm (sq. inch). For comparison, a five ton elephant standing on one leg would only produce a force of 350 kg (120 lb) per square cm (sq. inch) on the ground!

For chewing, the jaws are moved by powerful muscles at the side of the face.

Healthy gums

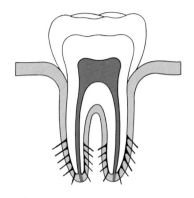

△ Tough ligaments help to bind the roots of a tooth firmly into its bony socket.

The gums are made up of tough rubbery tissue. It is attached tightly around the teeth, fitting snugly against the enamel crown of each tooth. The gum also covers the bone that keeps the teeth in place. Below the gum surface is the gum membrane that protects the softer dentin.

There are only a few places where there are gaps. Between the tooth and the gum is the **gingival crevice**, where leftover particles of food can become trapped. This is a danger area where germs or **bacteria** can collect. Bleeding or reddening gums are the first signs of problems. Any gum inflammation can also make it easier for bacteria to invade between the tooth and the gum, so proper dental care is very important.

The roots of the teeth fit into deep sockets in the bony jaw, but are not attached solidly to the bone. Instead they are surrounded by a thin layer of tissue, which is connected to the gum. The roots are firmly anchored by tough fibers called **ligaments.** The ligaments help to absorb the impact of biting and chewing and allow the tooth to shift slightly without becoming loose.

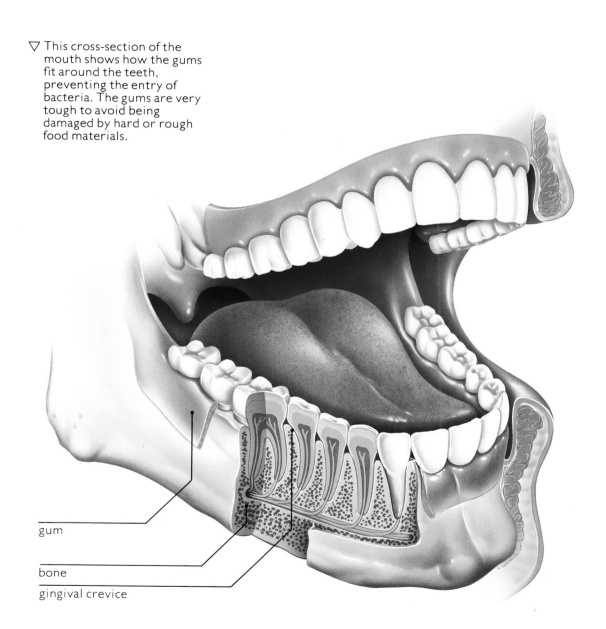

▽ This cross-section of the mouth shows how the gums fit around the teeth, preventing the entry of bacteria. The gums are very tough to avoid being damaged by hard or rough food materials.

gum

bone

gingival crevice

Plaque – the threat to gums and teeth

Most dental disease can be blamed on a colorless sticky layer called **plaque**, which forms over the teeth. It consists of billions of bacteria which live naturally in the mouth. This sticky layer absorbs dissolved food substances, providing nourishment for the bacteria.

Although a tooth's surface may seem smooth, it is actually pitted and fissured. Plaque collects in these tiny cracks, so however carefully you clean your teeth, there will always be some left to start the whole process again. Plaque builds up in the gaps between the teeth, which are difficult to brush clean. It also collects in the gingival crevice, where it forces the fleshy sealing tissue of the gum away from the teeth.

Plaque is a transparent, sticky layer which develops across the surface of the teeth. It is easily removed by careful brushing, but it tends to collect in the gaps between the teeth. If plaque is allowed to build up, it can push down into the gingival crevice alongside the teeth.

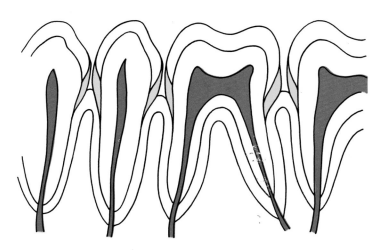

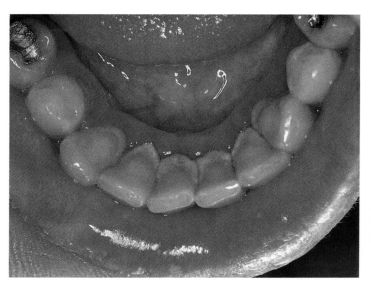

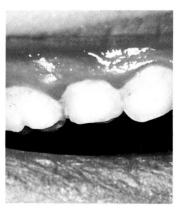

△ If plaque is not removed regularly, it gradually changes to hard, stony calculus, especially on the inside of the teeth.

▷ Plaque is not usually visible, but if it is present in very large amounts, as on this child's teeth, it can be seen as a yellowish deposit where the teeth enter the gums.

If plaque is not regularly removed by brushing, it can gradually harden to form **tartar** or **calculus**. This happens when minerals such as calcium, present in **saliva**, become deposited in the layer of plaque. A stony layer is produced which builds up to become unsightly and discolored. Its rough surface is impossible to keep clean and it can lead to gum disease and tooth loss as the calculus spreads below the gum surface.

Gum disease

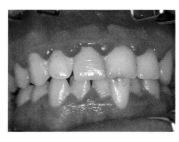

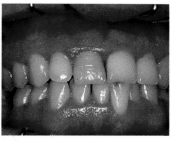

The top photograph shows gum disease or gingivitis. It has caused redness and swelling of the gums, which bleed when the teeth are cleaned.

The lower picture shows the same mouth, after the gingivitis has been treated properly. The gums are pink and healthy and should stay that way with proper mouth hygiene.

More teeth are lost through gum disease than from any other cause. The early stage of gum disease is called **gingivitis**. The first signs are red patches on the gums, which may bleed when you clean your teeth. To begin with it is not painful, but already damage is being done to your teeth and gums.

Gum disease is usually a direct result of the build-up of plaque and calculus which allows bacteria to infect the gum. As calculus accumulates in the pocket around the tooth, it forces the gum away. The calculus around the base of the tooth may become blackened due to blood leaking from the gum. Bacteria enter the damaged gum and can attack all the tissues around the tooth, including the ligaments which lock it in place.

If swollen gums are neglected, the infection can spread to the bone around the tooth socket, causing **periodontitis**. The bone is gradually destroyed, and the tooth becomes loose. It may eventually fall out.

The gums tend to shrink naturally in elderly people. This allows bacteria to enter and can loosen the teeth, so care of the gums is important at any age.

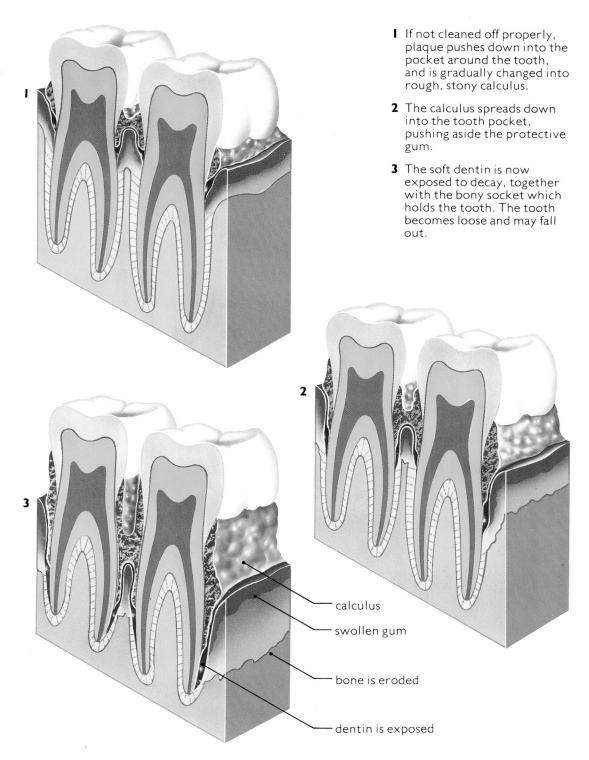

1 If not cleaned off properly, plaque pushes down into the pocket around the tooth, and is gradually changed into rough, stony calculus.

2 The calculus spreads down into the tooth pocket, pushing aside the protective gum.

3 The soft dentin is now exposed to decay, together with the bony socket which holds the tooth. The tooth becomes loose and may fall out.

calculus

swollen gum

bone is eroded

dentin is exposed

Sugar and dental health

We know that sugar, when allowed to remain in contact with the teeth for an extended period of time, promotes tooth decay. In countries where very little sugar is eaten, people have healthy teeth and gums even when they are very old.

This diagram shows how, just a few minutes after eating candy, the bacteria in the mouth are producing acid which attacks the tooth enamel. It also shows how conditions in the mouth remain acidic for quite some time before returning to normal.

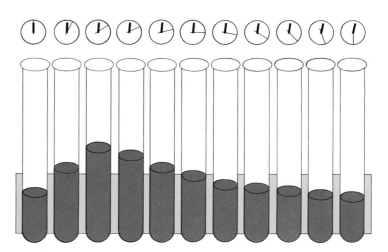

Sugar provides nourishment for the bacteria in plaque, enabling it to grow and spread. But when the bacteria use the sugar as food, acid is produced, which attacks the minerals in the tooth enamel. The enamel surface is softened, and this begins the process which leads to decay.

Our mouths have a natural defense mechanism to deal with acid. Our saliva is slightly alkaline and normally it neutralizes the acid in our mouths. But when the acid is locked inside the sticky layer of plaque, the saliva cannot wash it away quickly enough and it remains concentrated at the tooth surface.

When we eat sugar, in candies or in sweetened food or drinks, acid is produced and tooth enamel actually starts to dissolve. Even if no further sugar is consumed, it will take twenty to forty minutes before the acid is fully neutralized. So if you eat candy or consume sugary drinks frequently throughout the day, conditions in your mouth may stay acidic all day, causing continuous tooth damage. In fact, eating sweet things throughout the day is much more harmful than eating them only at proper meal times.

Dental decay

When acid attacks tooth enamel, it dissolves away patches of hard minerals, making the tooth surface spongy. This process usually begins in fissures in the tooth surface, or on the surfaces between the teeth, where it is difficult to clean.

At first the process is reversible. If you reduce the frequency of sugar in your diet and clean your teeth carefully to remove acid-forming plaque, the minerals will be slowly replaced from your saliva. But if the acid conditions persist, the area of softened enamel spreads and becomes deeper until there is a hole which reaches the dentin beneath. This material is much softer and is attacked even faster than enamel.

There are tiny nerve fibers in the dentin, so this is when toothache begins as the nerves are attacked by acid. Eventually the cavity penetrates right through to the pulp inside the tooth, allowing bacteria to flood in.

The inflamed pulp is trapped within the tooth. The infected tissue cannot swell, so pressure builds up, causing severe pain. The pressure may force the infected material out through the end of the root, causing a gum abscess.

1 The process of decay begins when acid attacks the enamel, making it porous and dissolving the surface.

2 Soon a hole or cavity develops, extending through the enamel and allowing acid to attack the soft dentin underneath. Once this stage is reached, decay will be fast.

3 Bacteria enter the porous dentin and soon reach the soft pulp inside the tooth. Here the bacteria will attack the blood vessels and nerves in the tooth cavity.

4 In the final stages of decay the pulp has been destroyed, and bacteria are leaking out into the tooth socket. A painful abscess develops, which may affect other teeth.

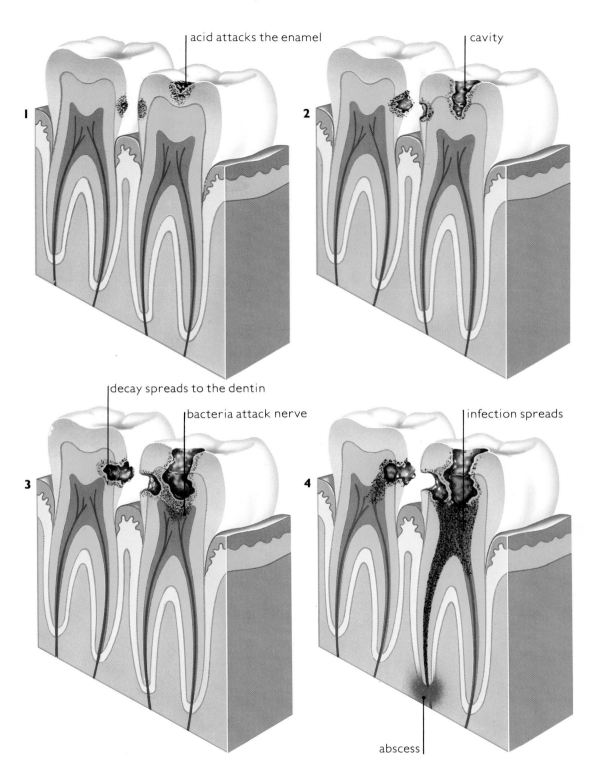

acid attacks the enamel

cavity

1

2

decay spreads to the dentin

bacteria attack nerve

3

4

infection spreads

abscess

Preventing tooth decay

The best way to prevent tooth decay is by frequent and proper brushing of your teeth. Brushing is not just to remove particles of food trapped between the teeth. The most important reason is to remove the layer of plaque that causes tooth decay.

Your dentist or oral hygienist will be able to advise you about the best way to clean your teeth properly. All methods involve working the bristles of the toothbrush between the teeth and into areas where plaque accumulates. Scrubbing or rolling movements help to dislodge the plaque.

To clean your teeth properly you must have a good, unworn toothbrush. The brush should have a small head to allow you to clean around inside your mouth and especially behind the teeth. Hard-bristled brushes can actually damage the teeth or gums, so choose a medium-grade brush which has nylon bristles with rounded ends. Always discard and replace your toothbrush as soon as it shows any signs of wear.

Toothpastes are mild abrasives which help the bristles to dislodge plaque. They also polish the tooth surface.

Dentists usually recommend a nylon-bristled brush with a small head, which is tilted to help clean behind the teeth. Specially shaped brushed are available to help you clean between the teeth to reach into awkward crevices.

26

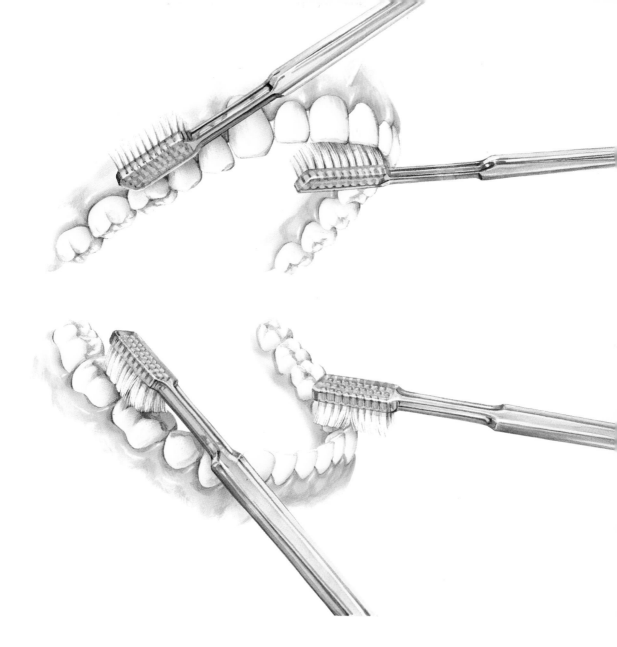

There are many recommended ways of cleaning the teeth, and your dentist will be able to advise on the method which is best for you. You should brush with small strokes. Don't just scrub to and fro. You won't clean between the teeth, and if you scrub too hard, you can actually wear grooves in the tooth enamel and damage your gums. Work the bristles of the brush thoroughly into the gaps between your teeth where plaque can lodge, as well as cleaning the fronts and the backs. Plaque can also gather in the cusps of the molar teeth. A rolling movement of the brush will help the bristles clean the tooth surface from all directions and get it completely clean.

Are your teeth really clean?

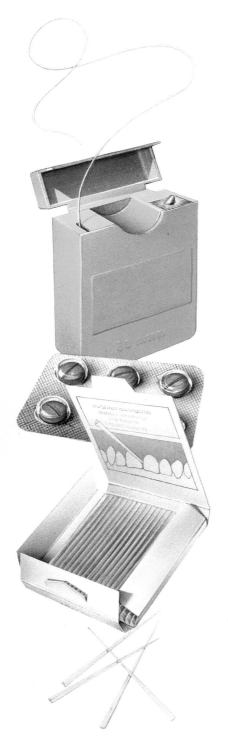

Even if you clean your teeth thoroughly, you may still be missing areas where damaging plaque accumulates. Because plaque is transparent, you won't know whether you have cleaned it all away. **Disclosing tablets** and solutions allow you to see where plaque is a problem. They contain harmless dyes which color the plaque (usually red or blue). If you use them *after* cleaning your teeth normally, you will find that certain areas of the tooth surface become brightly stained. You can then clean off the colored plaque with your toothbrush, remembering these danger areas each time you brush.

Everyone has some patches between the teeth where no toothbrush can reach. These areas are best cleaned with the help of **dental floss**.

▽ The easiest way to use dental floss is to tie a 30-cm (12-in) length into a loop and tighten it across the forefingers. You can then work it gently up and down between the gum and the teeth to dislodge trapped plaque. Be careful not to let it cut into your gums.

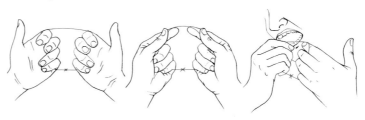

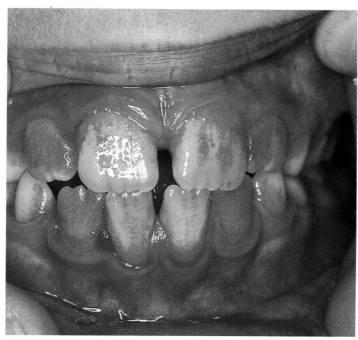

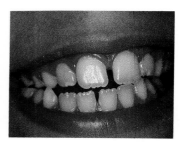

△ Because plaque is very difficult to see, the teeth here actually look quite clean.

◁ The same mouth after using disclosing tablets. Plaque on the teeth is brightly stained, showing the "danger" areas where extra care needs to be taken when cleaning the teeth.

Dental floss is thin thread made of artificial fibers. A length of floss is drawn between the teeth to dislodge plaque. Sometimes flossing causes the gums to bleed a little, but this usually only happens the first few times you use it.

The fluoride factor

In many places fluoride is added to the drinking water in very small amounts at water-purification plants. This helps protect the teeth from decay.

When teeth first erupt through the gums, they are hard and ready for use, but their structure is still slightly porous. Minerals from the saliva are slowly deposited in the surface layers of the enamel, making it tougher. We have already seen how these minerals can be attacked and dissolved. But there is a substance which can actually help to replace some of the minerals and harden the enamel. This is **fluoride**. Its useful property was first discovered by accident, when it was found that people suffered much less dental decay in areas where fluoride is naturally present in the water.

Fluoride not only strengthens the teeth. It also seems to discourage the activity of plaque bacteria by creating conditions in which they do not thrive. The protective action of fluoride is most effective in children, for it becomes deposited in the enamel as the teeth grow.

So how should we take advantage of fluoride? Most toothpastes now contain fluoride, and this is the easiest way to use it to protect your teeth. In some areas fluoride is added to the water in very small amounts, although elsewhere it may be present naturally. It can also be given in the form of drops or tablets, or as a solution which is painted on your teeth, but these are much stronger than the usual sources of fluoride, and need to be taken under supervision. Fluoride is now thought to be the single most important reason for improved dental health.

Most toothpastes now contain fluoride. Fluoride can also be taken in the form of tablets, drops and mouthwashes. To be most effective, fluoride should be taken from infancy. It is best to obtain your dentist's advice before taking extra fluoride, although the small amounts present in drinking water and toothpaste are perfectly safe.

31

Diet and healthy teeth

Sensible eating can help control tooth decay. All of the foods shown on this page are low in sugar, and therefore they don't encourage the production of acid which will attack tooth enamel. The foods and drinks on the opposite page are ones to avoid. They all contain sugar, which encourages the formation of acid.

Sugar is added to many prepared foods. It is also present in small quantities in many natural foods, such as fresh fruit, but in this form it is unlikely to cause much damage. If you eat sweet foods and drinks only at mealtimes, you will avoid decay provided you brush your teeth thoroughly afterwards.

It is the snacks, candies and sweet drinks between meals that are the real cause of the problem. And the longer the sugar stays in your mouth, the greater the damage it will cause. Constant chewing of sticky candy or sucking mints

throughout the day keeps acid levels in the mouth continuously high. Sipping sweetened drinks, including tea and coffee, has the same effect. Carbonated drinks are particularly harmful, since they contain acid as well as sugar. Even fruit juices can cause damage if you drink them in large quantities because of their high acid level.

If you do get hungry between meals, stick to snacks that don't contain sugar. Instead of cookies and candies, choose fresh fruit, raw vegetables such as carrots or celery, or nuts and seeds.

How the dentist can help

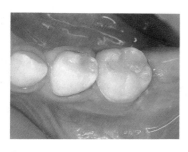

Early attention to the teeth can prevent worse trouble later on. The biting surfaces of these teeth had developed small cracks, which have been sealed with a clear, tough plastic material to prevent the entry of acid or bacteria.

Opposite

A regular check-up at the dentist helps you to be sure that you are looking after your teeth properly.

If you brush your teeth thoroughly, and use fluoride toothpaste, why should you need to visit the dentist regularly?

The most important reason is to prevent problems before they arise. Your dentist will be able to check behind and in between your teeth to find hidden decay, as well as detecting the first signs of damage to the enamel. Using thin probes, the dentist can feel damage in even the most inaccessible gaps between the teeth, and decide whether treatment is needed.

Your dentist may also refer you to a dental hygienist for some general "maintenance" work on your teeth. The hygienist will make sure you are cleaning your teeth properly and check that your gums are healthy. The dentist or hygienist may also "scale and polish" your teeth to remove any build-up of calculus. This simply involves scraping the calculus away. The teeth are then polished with a mild abrasive to remove any remaining deposits or stains. If there is damage to the enamel, a special liquid may be painted on to the teeth. This seals small cracks or chips and prevents the entry of bacteria.

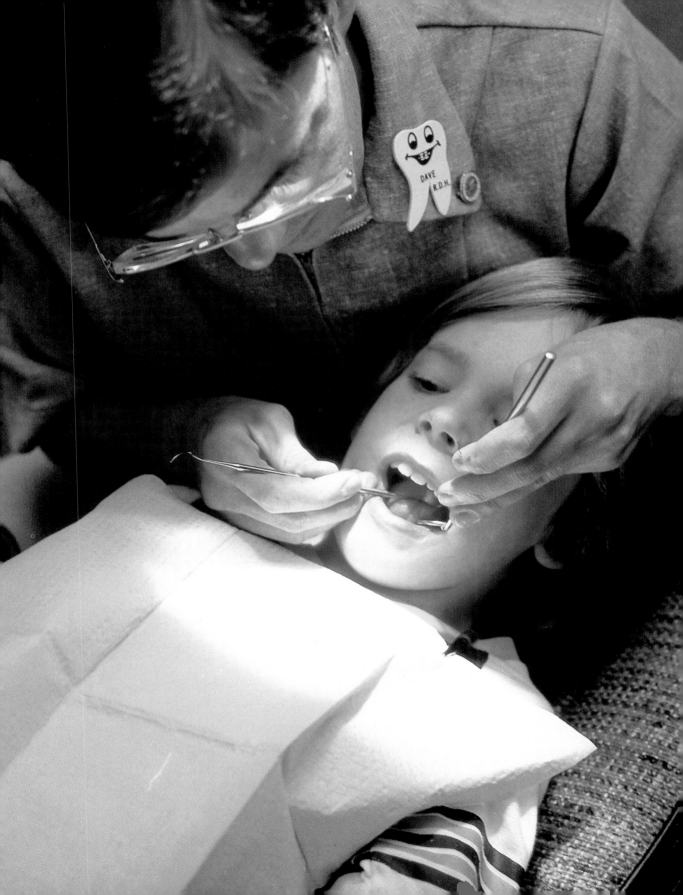

Filling the gap

1 Often the small hole on the surface of a decayed tooth does not give any idea of the amount of damage beneath.

2 The dentist must remove all the decayed tooth around the cavity.
The cavity is thoroughly cleaned and dried before being packed with the permanent filling. This is then shaped to match the surface of the tooth.

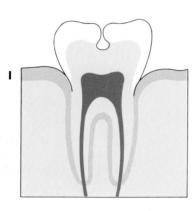

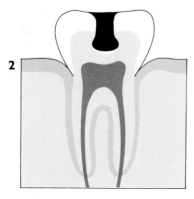

If your dentist finds a cavity, it will need to be filled to prevent further decay. The dentist will usually take an **X ray**, which shows exactly how far the damage has spread.

The dentist will give you an injection in your gum near the tooth that is to be filled. This numbs the tooth and gum so you won't feel any pain.

First all the decayed part of the tooth must be removed before the filling is put in. The dentist uses a tiny drill to grind away all the decayed enamel and dentin. The cavity is always made larger than the opening on to the surface of the tooth, so that the filling will not drop out.

Fillings may be made of **amalgam**, a mixture of metals with mercury, or of a white plastic material which blends in with the tooth. The filling material is packed firmly into the cleaned cavity. The dentist smooths the surface of the filling before it hardens.

If decay has penetrated right into the pulp cavity, the dentist removes all of the soft interior of the tooth. The tooth is then filled with a packing substance to prevent the entry of bacteria. Finally the cavity is packed with a normal filling.

1 In an X-ray photograph materials which block the rays appear white. In this picture a lower molar has been fitted with a metal crown, while above it a cavity in the side of a tooth has been filled with amalgam.

2 In this picture there are two small filled cavities in the biting surface of a molar.

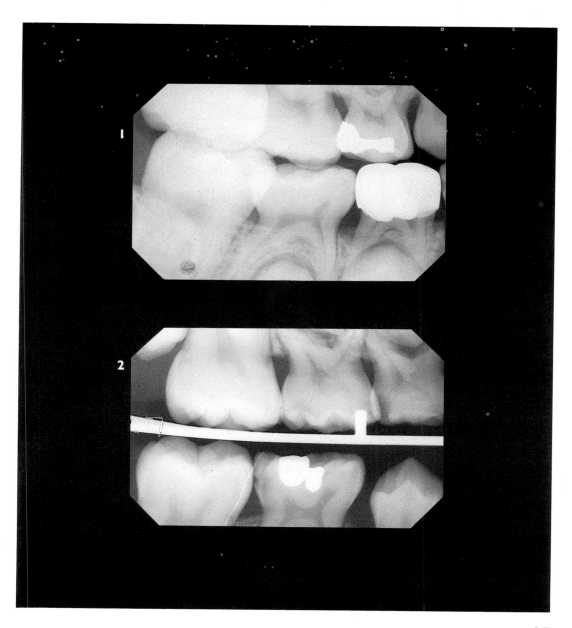

As good as new?

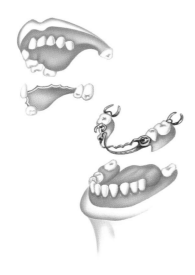

Sometimes a tooth may be too badly decayed to be filled. The dentist may then recommend fitting a **crown** to the tooth. This is an artificial replacement for all or part of a tooth. Crowns can also be fitted if a tooth is broken or if a person is very self-conscious about misshapen or permanently discolored teeth.

△ Dentures are made of plastic, which is molded and shaped to fit the upper or lower gums. They may replace all of the teeth, or just those which have been removed. Some forms of dentures clip around the remaining teeth with springy wires.

The dentist grinds away much of the tooth, and into this inserts a small metal post. The stump is covered by a temporary tooth while a proper porcelain replacement is made. This has to be carefully matched to the color of the patient's teeth. The new tooth is bonded on to the stump or metal post with very strong dental cement. It should last for many years, and the new tooth will look just like the natural teeth.

▽ An artificial crown can be fitted to repair a damaged tooth. Sometimes a larger bridge is inserted, when the new tooth is braced against nearby teeth.

If several teeth have been lost, the dentist may fit dentures – a common procedure in the elderly and, unfortunately, in many young people. The dentist gets the patient to bite into a pad of soft material which gives an exact impression of the gums and remaining teeth. From this, dentures can be constructed which will fit around the remaining teeth or replace all the teeth.

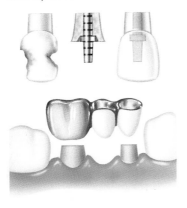

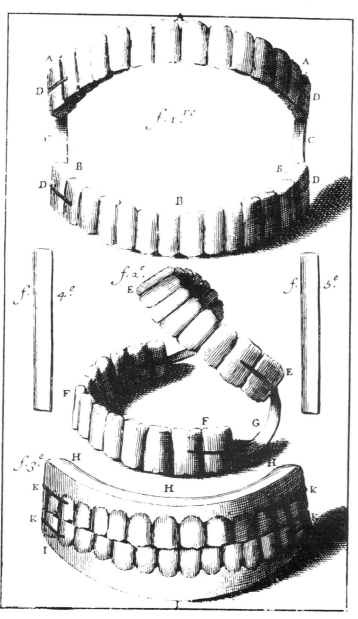

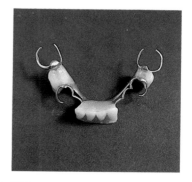

△ This partial denture has been made to clip around the remaining teeth at the back of the jaw. It is smaller and more convenient than the old-fashioned full dentures.

◁ There is nothing new about artificial teeth. Dentures have been made for centuries. Originally they were constructed of ivory or bone, but examples in wood have also been found. They must have looked terrible!

A helping hand for the teeth

Not everyone has perfect teeth, and much dental treatment is carried out to make teeth look better. This is called **orthodontics**.

If one or other parent has poorly aligned teeth, it is likely that their children's teeth will be similar. Thumb or finger sucking in childhood often causes teeth to stick out. Although teeth are firmly sunk into the jaw, they can move, very slowly, if pressure is applied to them over a long period.

An orthodontist can straighten teeth by fixing a brace over them. Over a period of up to eighteen months, the tooth gradually moves. The orthodontist adjusts the brace occasionally to keep constant pressure on the tooth. Sometimes such a brace is wired to nearby teeth. Often it is a small device which can be taken out of the mouth for cleaning.

Sometimes there is not enough room in the jaw for all the teeth. The adult teeth overlap and grow crooked as they come through the gums. The dentist may decide to remove one or more teeth. The teeth will soon rearrange themselves on the gum.

This girl is wearing a modern orthodontic brace to encourage her teeth to take up the proper position in her jaw. She will have to wear it for several months, but afterwards, her teeth will be well positioned and healthy. Such braces need to be checked and adjusted at intervals.

Extraction or repair

In medieval times dentistry was carried out by barber-surgeons, who also cut hair, shaved patients and set broken bones.

Dentists always try to save a tooth whenever possible. But when a tooth is decayed or damaged beyond repair, it may be necessary to extract it. Extractions are carried out under an injection or **anesthetic**, so you don't feel any pain. There are seldom any bad aftereffects, either. Most people are glad to have got rid of a tooth which may have been causing them pain for a considerable time.

After a few days, the tissue covering the gums grows over the socket. The inflammation clears up, leaving the gum smooth and healthy.

Sometimes a tooth gets knocked out or broken accidentally. With a broken or chipped tooth, you must consult the dentist as soon as possible to see if a crown should be fitted. Act quickly before decay sets in. If the tooth is knocked out completely, wrap the tooth in cool damp tissue, then go to the dentist quickly.

A more common dental emergency is when a filling drops out or a crown comes loose. There is little that can be done except to contact your dentist as soon as possible.

△ Accidents can sometimes occur in sports like BMX racing and hockey. For many such sports it is advisable to wear some form of mouth protection, as damage to the front teeth can be both painful and unsightly.

▷ In the past tooth extraction was very painful and not very skillful. It was often caricatured but was not funny for the sufferers. Visiting the dentist today is no longer an ordeal, and if treatment is needed it is quick and painless.

The future

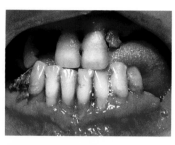

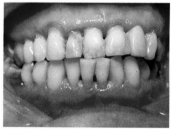

These two pictures show the benefits of proper dental care. The top picture shows the neglected teeth of a 20-year-old man. They are decayed and discolored, and his gums are also diseased. The lower picture shows the mouth of an 80-year-old woman with a full set of teeth which are only lightly discolored. This just shows it can be done!

What will the future bring for dental health? There are already moves being made to reduce the amount of sugar in our diets. This means that dental decay caused by sugar will be much less common than it is today. Almost all toothpaste now contains fluoride, so people of all ages can benefit from the additional protection against tooth decay.

Once many people in their twenties lost their teeth because they could not afford regular dental treatment or were frightened of going to the dentist. Now all that has changed. Dental treatment is available to everyone and regular check-ups are now a normal part of people's lives. New developments in anesthetics and high-speed drills mean that dental treatment need not be painful. Orthodontic treatment is becoming more important as people realize that if teeth are going to last a lifetime, they should look good and be healthy.

Scientists are already testing **vaccines** that could help the body to resist the acid-forming bacteria living in plaque. If these prove successful, tooth decay could become a thing of the past.

The dental hygienist will advise you how to keep your teeth and gums healthy. With proper care your teeth should last a lifetime.

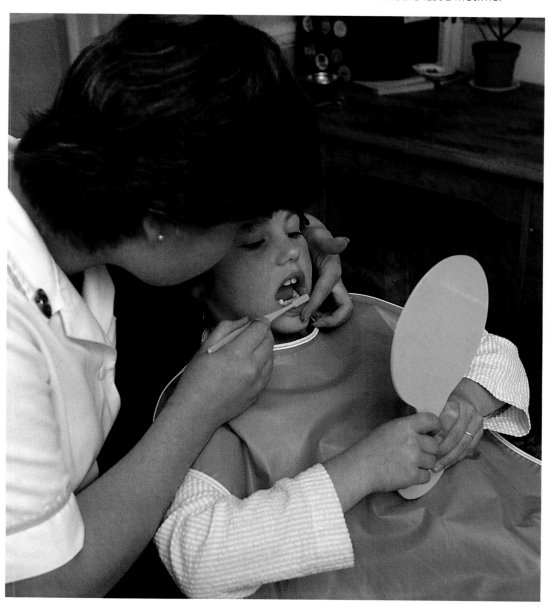

Glossary

Acid: substance produced in the mouth by the action of bacteria living in plaque. Acid softens and attacks the tooth enamel, beginning the process which leads to cavities and decay.

Amalgam: material used to fill cavities. It is a mixture of metals which sets hard after being packed into the cleaned cavity.

Anesthetic: substance which prevents the sensation of pain. Most dental anesthetics are given as injections which numb the tooth and gum. Sometimes a general anesthetic is given so that complicated dental work can be carried out while the patient is unconscious.

Bacteria: microscopic organisms present in the mouth in large numbers. They produce acid which attacks the teeth and can cause tooth decay and gum disease.

Brace: a simple device which puts pressure on a misplaced tooth so that it moves to its proper position in the gum.

Bridge: a replacement tooth, or teeth, attached to healthy teeth at either side.

Calcium: hard stony material which gives the teeth their strength.

Calculus: also known as tartar. Rough stony deposit on the teeth which builds up if the teeth are not brushed properly.

Canines: pointed teeth at the sides of the mouth which are used to tear food. They are larger and more important in some meat-eating animals.

Carnivore: an animal which eats meat.

Cavity: a hole in a tooth made by acid. It is the first stage of tooth decay.

Crown: the part of the tooth which shows above the gum. The term is also used to describe an artificial tooth fitted over the base of a decayed tooth.

Cusp: sharp pointed projection on the biting surface of a tooth, used for grinding food.

Decay: process in which teeth are damaged by acid produced by bacteria.

Dental floss: specially treated thread. It is worked between the teeth to dislodge plaque which cannot be reached by brushing.

Dentin: the spongy material inside a tooth, beneath the enamel layer. Dentin is easily attacked by acid and bacteria when a cavity develops.

Dentures: artificial or false teeth.

Disclosing tablets: harmless tablets of dye which color plaque brightly so it can easily be seen.

Enamel: the hard and smooth outer covering of a tooth.

Fluoride: substance which, in very small amounts, can help the tooth resist decay. It is often added to toothpaste and drinking water.

Gingival crevice: small crease in the gum, formed where the tooth emerges. It is from here that gum disease develops.

Gingivitis: gum disease; an inflammation of the gums.

Gum: the tough rubbery covering over the jaw bone.

Incisors: sharp flat cutting teeth at the front of the mouth.

Ligament: tough string-like material which binds the tooth into its socket in the jaw bone.

Milk teeth: also known as the deciduous teeth, these are the first teeth to appear through the gums in early childhood. They are shed and replaced during the teens.

Molar: broad grinding tooth at the back of the jaw.

Nerve: fiber which conveys sensation from the tooth to the brain.

Orthodontics: treatment of badly positioned teeth.

Oxygen: gas breathed from the air which is necessary for life for all cells of the body.

Periodontitis: very severe gum disease which also affects the tooth socket.

Plaque: sticky transparent layer over the teeth, containing millions of bacteria. Plaque is responsible for tooth decay

Premolar: also known as a bicuspid. This is a grinding tooth positioned between the canine and molar teeth.

Pulp cavity: the hollow within the tooth, containing nerves and blood vessels.

Root: the base of the tooth which fits into a socket in the jaw bone.

Saliva: watery secretion which helps lubricate the food as it is chewed and swallowed. Substances in the saliva are deposited on the teeth to form calculus.

Sealant: material which is painted on to a tooth to fill and cover small cracks or pits, preventing the development of decay.

Tartar: see calculus.

Vaccine: Harmless or dead bacteria, given to encourage the body to fight off an infection. Vaccines are being developed to help prevent tooth decay.

Wisdom teeth: the last four molars to appear at the back of the jaws, usually in the late teens. Sometimes they never break through and may need to be removed.

X ray: process which allows the dentist to photograph the teeth and show up any hidden damage or decay.

Index

PRINTED IN BELGIUM BY
proost
INTERNATIONAL BOOK PRODUCTION